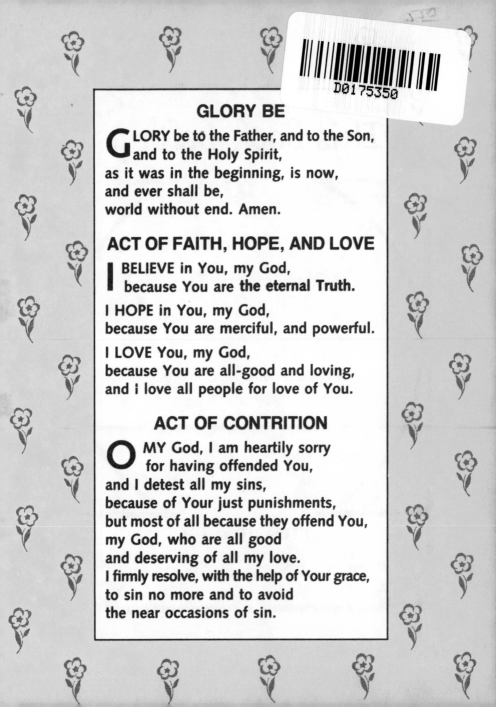

GLORY BE

GLORY be to the Father, and to the Son,
and to the Holy Spirit,
as it was in the beginning, is now,
and ever shall be,
world without end. Amen.

ACT OF FAITH, HOPE, AND LOVE

I BELIEVE in You, my God,
because You are the eternal Truth.

I HOPE in You, my God,
because You are merciful, and powerful.

I LOVE You, my God,
because You are all-good and loving,
and i love all people for love of You.

ACT OF CONTRITION

O MY God, I am heartily sorry
for having offended You,
and I detest all my sins,
because of Your just punishments,
but most of all because they offend You,
my God, who are all good
and deserving of all my love.
I firmly resolve, with the help of Your grace,
to sin no more and to avoid
the near occasions of sin.

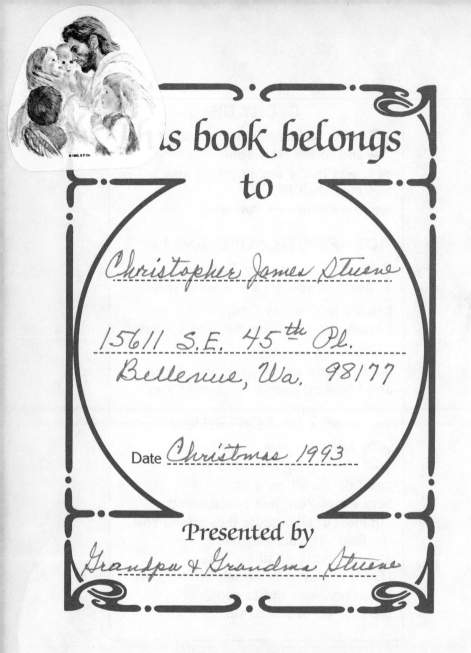

This book belongs to

Christopher James Struen

15611 S.E. 45th Pl.
Bellevue, Wa. 98177

Date Christmas 1993

Presented by

Grandpa & Grandma Struen

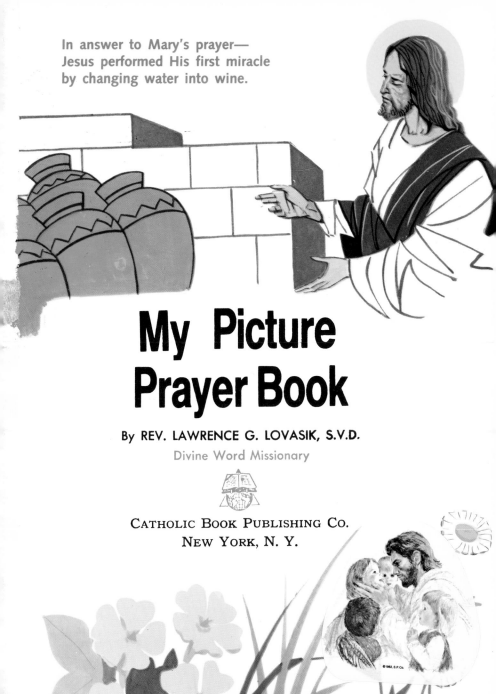

In answer to Mary's prayer—
Jesus performed His first miracle
by changing water into wine.

My Picture
Prayer Book

By REV. LAWRENCE G. LOVASIK, S.V.D.

Divine Word Missionary

CATHOLIC BOOK PUBLISHING CO.
NEW YORK, N. Y.

My Morning Prayer

My heavenly Father,
I thank You for this new day.
May I live it all for You
as Your good and loving child.

Whatever may happen to me this day,
I offer it all to You,
and thank You for what may make me happy,
or what may make me sad.

I know that You watch over me,
and love me in everything You send.

Dear Father,
keep me close to Your loving Heart,
and always be my Father.
I love You more than I can say.

2

NIHIL OBSTAT: Daniel V. Flynn, J.C.D., *Censor Librorum*

IMPRIMATUR: ✠ Joseph T. O'Keefe, *Vicar Gen., New York Archdiocese*

God, the Creator

God, You made all things:
the sun, the sea and rivers,
the hills and mountains, valleys,
trees, and everything that grows.

I thank You for all the beauty
You have given us in this world.

All this makes me remember
that You have created me
and want me to love and serve You
and reach my heavenly home.

God, You made all things.
I worship You as my Lord
and my Creator,
and I am happy to call You Father.

3

Lord, Take All That I Am

Lord Jesus Christ,
take all that I am:
my memory, my mind, and my will.

All that I have and love
You have given me.

I give it all back to You
to be guided by Your will.

I trust in You:
let me love You more.

I am sorry for my sins:
give me a greater sorrow for them.

I want to do what You ask of me:
in the way You ask,
for as long as You ask,
because You ask it.

Lord, give light to my mind,
and strength to my will;
make my body pure
and my soul holy.

4

My God, You Are My Hope

My God, You are my hope and my strength,
Without You I would fall.
Keep me in the bright light of Your truth
and guide me on my way each day.

God, my Father,
each day You show me Your love
and give me Your Holy Spirit,
to live within me.

I thank You for the gifts of love
I have received from the Heart of Jesus,
Your Son and my Redeemer.
Open my heart to share His life
and please keep blessing me with His love.

Father, I have hurt the Heart of Jesus
by my many sins,
but I ask You to forgive me.
Help me to show that I really love You,
and to make up for my sins.

My Night Prayer

I thank You, Lord,
for having been with me all this day.
I thank You for the many good things
You have done for me.

I ask You to forgive me
for anything I have done wrong.
I know that You love me all the more
if I am truly sorry.

Keep me in Your loving care this night.

Continued on next page

6

Bless my dear mother and father
and my brothers and sisters
and all those who are kind to me.
Help us all to love You more
and serve You well tomorrow.

When our life is over
take our family to Yourself
and let us be together again
in Your heavenly glory!

A Prayer for Our Family

My heavenly Father,
through the prayer of Mary,
the virgin Mother of God
and of her husband Joseph,
protect our family,
my mother and father,
my brothers and sisters.
Help us to live in peace with You
and one another.

Help us to follow the example
of the holy Family of Your
beloved Son
in love and respect,
and bring us to the joy and peace
of Your heavenly home.
I ask this through the prayers
of Jesus, Mary, and Joseph.

For My Mother and Father

Dear God,
I love to call You "Father."
Thank You for being so good to me.
Thank You for giving me a mother and father
to love and care for me.

Keep my father safe
when he goes to work each day.
Bless him for giving us a home
and clothes and food
and many other good things.

Bless my mother, too,
for all her love for me.
Help me to make her happy
by giving her my love.

Thank You, God, for Fruit

Thank You, God,
for all the good things
You give us to eat:
fruit, vegetables, and grains,
and other good food.

You take care of us
as our loving Father.
May all Your gifts to us
help us to remember Your love,
and love You in return.

I pray for all the hungry people
all over the world,
who do not have the food
and other good things
which You have given me.
Give them food, dear Lord,
and lead them close to You.

Thank You, God, for Flowers

Thank You, God,
for giving us this wonderful world
to look at and enjoy.

I thank You for the flowers and grass,
for the trees and bushes
that grow all around us.
They make us think of You
and how beautiful You are.

When I look at flowers in many colors,
which only You can make,
may I remember to thank You
for being my loving Father
and for giving me a heart and soul
to tell You how much I love You.

Thank You, God,
for Animals

Thank You, God, for all the
  animals
that You have made
to be our friends on earth,
and even to be our food.
Without them we could not live.

Thank You for the pets I have
to make me happy each day.
You made them to be my
  companions.
They, too, are gifts of Your love,
because You want to see me
  happy.

12

Continued on next page.

Thank You, God my Creator,
for giving me a soul and body.
You made me so much greater
than all the animals on earth.

I want to know and love and serve You,
and be with You in heaven someday.

Lord, Thanks for My Pets

My heavenly Father,
You take care of every creature
because You give life
to all things that live.

You have made animals
to be our companions in life.

Thank You for giving me pets
which give me such great joy.

Let me be kind to all animals,
because they are Your gift to us.

14

God, Thank You
for Your Care

God, You told Noah to build an ark,
and to take into it a pair
of very many animals.
You then sent rains for forty days
which flooded the earth.
But You saved Noah and his family,
and all the animals.

Your care for Noah and his family
teaches us how You love our families.
Your care for the animals
teaches us that we must respect
all Your creatures
and use them as You have commanded
    us.

God, thank You for Your loving care.

15

God, Thank You for the Sun

Dear God in heaven,
thank You for the sun which You made
to give us light, energy, and warmth.

Grant me the light of Your faith,
the energy of Your grace,
and the warmth of Your love.

Thank You for the beautiful sky,
for the fields and woods,
for the flowers and plants and birds.
All these are Your gift to me
to give me joy.

What the sun is to the earth,
that You are to me, my God.
I cannot live without You.

Thank You, God, for Fire

Lord, our God,
You take care of us in all our needs
because You love us.

Thank You for giving us fire,
to give us light when it is dark,
to keep us warm when it is cold,
and to cook our meals when we are
    hungry.

May fire remind me
of the warmth of Your love for me,
and of the Holy Spirit
Who lives in my soul by His grace.

May He fill my heart
with the fire of His love.

God, Thank You for Water

God, my heavenly Father,
I thank You for water:
for the sea, brooks, and rivers.
Thank You for the many kinds of fish
   and frogs
that live in lakes and ponds.

Thank You for the fish
which we can catch and eat,
and all the wonderful creatures
that live in water.

Thank You for giving us water to drink;
without it we would die.

Lord, how useful water is!
We use so much of it every day —
to drink, and cook,
and wash, and play.

Thank You for the rain
that makes things grow
to give us food.

20

Father, Thank You for the Seasons

Heavenly Father,
I thank You for all the seasons
of the year
and for all the wonderful things they bring.

I thank You for the lesson of the seasons.
They come and go in order till the year is over,
only to begin again the next year.
So my life has begun and will end someday.
I must prepare for the eternal life of heaven.
One year will be my last.
Then take me home to You, dear Father.

21

Thank You, Father,
for Letting Me Love You

My heavenly Father,
if You take care of things in nature:
plants, butterflies, insects and birds,
flowers and trees and grass,
how much more will You take care of
    me,
Your little child.

The beautiful things on earth
praise Your power and give You glory.
But only I can really know You
and love You with all my heart.
Only I and people who serve You well
can know and love and praise You
in heaven someday.

Father, Thank You
for My Food

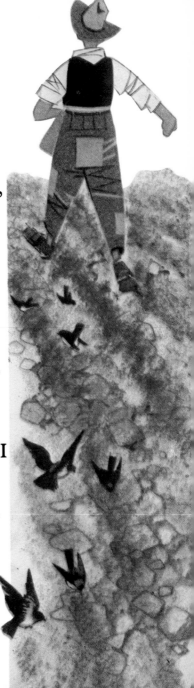

Father in heaven,
You take care of us, Your children,
by giving us the food we need
that we might live.

The farmer plants the seed,
and You bless his crop.
You send rain and sunshine
and the grain grows high
that we might have bread to eat.

Father, thank You for my food.
Let me show my love for You
by trusting You for everything I
    need.

Please help those who are hungry
in the whole world.

23

Thank You, Lord,
for Fruit

Heavenly Father,
You have given us the food we
   need.

You have made all kinds of good
   fruits
for us to enjoy.

I think about apples, oranges,
cherries, plums, grapes, and
   bananas.

All kinds of fruits give us good
   food
to keep us healthy and strong
and to make us grow.

Thank You, Father,
for giving us tasty fruits.

Thank You, Lord, for Rest

My heavenly Father,
thank You for the body
You have made for me.
You want me to take good care of it
and keep it healthy.

After a busy day of work and play,
my body is tired and I need rest.

Thank You for the night's rest
You give me,
which makes me strong again
to begin another day.

Each night I place myself
into Your loving arms
that You may protect me
and give me a good night's rest.

Thank You, Lord, for my rest.

Thank You, God, for My Home

God, my loving Father,
I thank You for my home
where I spend most of my life,
and where my parents and family
show me their love.

Thank You for the things I like at
    home,
where I spend so many happy hours
with those I love very much.

Thank You for the home that
    protects me
in heat and cold and rain,
and where I work and sleep and play;
where I talk, laugh, eat, and drink;
where so many wonderful things
happen to me, and where I am safe.

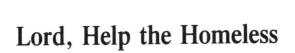

Lord, Help the Homeless

Lord, I am glad I have a home
where I live with people I love,
and who love me also.

But there are many children
who do not have a home
because they are too poor.

Some are homeless and lonesome
because they have no parents,
or have lost their home
because of war, or floods
or earthquakes.

Lord, please help all those children
and all people who need a home
and food and clothes.

Lord, Be My Teacher

Lord, we come to school each day
    to learn.
Help me to work well and study
    hard.
Make our school a happy place
where we can learn the things
that will help us in life,
and where we can enjoy ourselves.

Bless all my teachers
who spend their time with me.

Lord, I want You to be my Teacher,
that I may learn
the important things of life:
to know and love and serve You
and reach my heavenly home.

Continued on next page

Lord, teach me all the
   things
I must learn in school,
that tell me about the
   world You made.

You want me to be
   happy
in using the things I learn
and be able to help others
to be happy also.

Jesus, I offer You
all my school-work
and I ask You to bless it
that it may be pleasing
   to God.

Jesus, Bless My Teachers

Jesus, Your Mother Mary
and good St. Joseph were Your teachers,
when You were a child like me.
You listened to them carefully
and did everything they told You to do.

Help me to be attentive in school
and to do my homework well.

Help me always to study hard
to please my parents and teachers,
but especially to please You.

Jesus, bless my teachers
who work so hard for me
to teach me the things I must know
to make my life happy.

Continued on next page

Lord, bless the teachers
who teach me religion.

Send me Your Holy Spirit
to give light to my mind
that I may know the meaning
of all that my priests and teachers
tell me about You
and all You have done for us.

I want to study hard
the lessons of my Catholic Faith
that I may live a good Christian life
and save my soul.

Jesus, be my Teacher.
You are the Way,
the Truth,
and the Life.
Help me to listen to You!

Thank You, Lord, for Toys and Playmates

Jesus, when You were a child
I know You played with toys
    as I do.
You also played games with
    Your friends.

Lord Jesus, thank You
for the toys my parents
and good friends have bought for
    me.

Bless all my playmates.
Do not let me be selfish in
    my games.
I want to share my toys with
    others,
and make them happy, too.

Continued on next page

Keep me from getting angry
and using bad words.
Never let me fight with others
or always want to have my own
way.

I am sorry for making my playmates unhappy
because of the way I act.

Be with us in the games we play
that we may please You
in everything we do.

Bless the fun we have
that it may get us ready
to work all the harder for You.

Lord, Thanks for Television

Lord, You know how much fun
 I have
watching television.
I also learn a lot,
and enjoy good stories and
 cartoons.

Thank You for all the actors,
singers, musicians, and dancers,
and the beautiful scenes of nature
 in color.

Lord, please keep me from
 watching
the things I should not see or hear.
Let television make me a better
 person
and not do me any harm.

God Thank You for Your Presents

God, my Father,
thank You for the many things You
  give me
to make me very happy.

You have given me life:
I can run and skip and jump.
I can laugh and sing
and read and write, paint and sew.
I can think and learn
and enjoy beautiful music.

There are so many things I can do—
thank You for these wonderful
  presents.
I want to praise You always
by using them well.

Lord, Thank You for My Friends

Jesus, when You were young like me
You, too, had many friends.
I am sure they all loved You
because You were always kind.

Teach me how to be kind to my friends
who do nice things for me.

Continued on next page.

36

Let me share with them the
    things I have,
and try to make them happy.

I am sorry if I have hurt them
    by what I said or did.

Bless my friends and keep
    them good.
Give them good health and all
    they need,
and many blessings from
    heaven.
Guide them through their
    lives
with Your Mother's help.

Reward them for all the joy
they daily bring to me.
Bring them all to heaven
where we shall be happy
    forever.

Thank You, Lord,
    for each day,
for fun, for friends,
and work and play.
Thank You, Lord,
    for Your loving care.

Father, Thank You for Joy

Heavenly Father,
by the death of Your Son
and by His glorious rising again,
You have redeemed us.

Grant me grace to keep from sin.
Make me live each day
in the joy of the Resurrection of
    Jesus.

You made me Your child in Christ.
Free me from sin
and bring me the joy that lasts for
    ever.
May I have the joy
the risen Jesus has won for me.

Bring me to a joyous life in You
through my daily prayers,
and through Your offering in the
    Mass
and Holy Communion that You
    give me.

38

God, Bless My Grandparents

Thank You, Lord, for giving me grandparents,
who love me as my parents do,
and give me things to show they care
and want me to be good.

Do not leave them alone
now that they are old and gray.
Watch over them
as they move slowly along toward You.

Make people kind to them
and help them when they can.

Thank You for the good things
You have done for them.

I want to make them happy
and always pray for them,
because their love for me in life
makes me think of Your love for me.

Jesus, You Died
on the Cross for Me

Jesus, You are the Lamb of God.
You took away the sins of the world
by dying on the Cross for us.
You destroyed death and gave us
    new life.
I offer You my prayer of love.

Jesus, You were without sin,
and yet You suffered for us sinners.
By Your death on the Cross
You brought us forgiveness of our
    sins.
By Your rising from the dead
You have raised us up to a holy life
of grace and peace and love.

In Your mercy, save my soul,
which You bought with Your own
    Blood,
when You died on the Cross for me.
Through Your love for me,
bring me to eternal life in heaven.

Father, Forgive Me

Our Father in heaven:
Please forgive me for the things
I have done wrong;
for angry words and bad temper;
for being greedy
and wanting the best for myself;
for making other people unhappy.

My loving Father,
I love You
because You are so good.
I am sorry for all my sins
and all I have done to hurt You.

With the help of Your grace,
I will try to do better
that I may please You
and show You my love.

Make me one with You always,
so that my joy may be holy,
and honor You by helping others
for the love of You.
Bring me the joy that lasts forever.

Father, Thank You for Peace

Heavenly Father,
by dying on the Cross for love
of us
Your dear Son Jesus
brought peace to the world.

All that is good comes from You
and brings peace to my heart.
Give me the peace
of loving and serving You.

I pray for the peace
which this world does not give.

May the power of Your love
guide me in all I do
to please You in all things.

Fill me with Your Holy Spirit
and make me one with You
in peace and love.

Father, thank You for Your
peace.

Jesus, Thanks for Christmas

Jesus, Christmas trees
make me think of Christmas
when You became a child like me
to show Your love for me
and for all people.

Jesus, Christmas trees
make me think of eternal life,
which You came to bring us.
As the Christmas tree is always fresh
    and green,
so may my good deeds and Your grace
lead me to eternal life with You.

Jesus, thanks for Christmas
that brought You to me —
the greatest Gift of all!

Little Infant, I love You

Little Jesus, lying in the crib,
with Mary and Joseph I adore You.
With the shepherds who came to see You,
I give You my love and my life.
I offer all that I have and am
as the best gift I can give You,
at Christmas, and always!
Little Infant Jesus, I love You, God and Man!

Lord, Make My Life a Song of Praise

Jesus, when You were born,
the angels sang:
"Glory to God in the highest,
and peace on earth
to men of good will!"

Like the angels,
I want to praise You all my life.
I want to sing Your glory
in all my thoughts and words
    and deeds.
May my whole life
be a song of praise to You.

God the Father,
thank You for creating me.
God the Son,
thank You for redeeming me.
God the Holy Spirit,
thank You for making me
    holy.

Father, Bless Our Family

Lord Jesus,
You came among us as a man,
to lead us from darkness
into the light of faith.
Through baptism we became children
of Your heavenly Father.
In Your love for us all,
You give us Your sacraments
to lift us up to eternal life.

Father in heaven,
help our family to live like the holy
Family,
Jesus, Mary, and Joseph.
Through the prayers of Mary,
the virgin Mother of God,
and of her husband, Joseph,
fill our hearts with peace and love.

Give us strength to face
the troubles of this life.
Bring us to Your eternal home
in heaven.

Continued on next page

Father in heaven,
bless our family
and keep us close
to You —
with Jesus, Mary,
and Joseph.

47

Father,
Teach Me
How to Pray

God, my loving Father,
teach me how to pray to You.
I want to tell You about the things
that worry me or make me afraid,
and about the things
that make me happy
and fill my life with joy.

Continued on next page.

When I pray You speak to me, too.
Help me to listen carefully
that I may know more about You
and the things You want me to do.

It is good to know that You are with
me
in the temple of my soul,
because through Baptism I became Your
child,
and You live in me through Your grace.

Be my Friend, dear God,
and listen to my prayers
when I ask for Your help to be good,
or for blessing on my parents,
my brothers and sisters and friends.

Thank You, Lord,
for the Gift of Life

I thank You, Lord, for the life
You have given me through my parents.

I thank You for my eyes,
to see all the things that are beautiful
in this wonderful world You made.

I thank You for my mind,
to know what is true
and to think of You
and all You really are.

I thank You for my heart and will,
to love what is good —
to love You, the Greatest Good.

God, my Creator,
You have given me a body and soul.

Thank You for the gift of divine life —
Your own life which You first gave me
in the Sacrament of Baptism.

Thank You for the many graces
You give me through Your Sacraments,
which help me to know and love
and serve You as Your child.

52 *Continued on next page*

My God,
I thank You for Your love.
May my love for You
show itself in all I do,
for I always want to please
    You
as Jesus did on earth.
I want to do good for others
because I love You,
because we are all Your
    children
and have been redeemed by
    the Blood of Jesus on the
    Cross.

Give me strength and joy
in serving You as a follower of
    Christ.

May the hand of Your loving
    kindness
guide me each moment of
    each day.
Forgive my sins, and keep me
    in Your peace.
Lead me to my home in
    heaven.

Thank You, Lord, for the Eucharist

Jesus, thank You for the gift of Yourself
which You left us at the Last Supper.

I believe that in the Mass You offer again
the sacrifice of Your life on the Cross,
but now without shedding Your Blood,
for You are the Risen Lord.

I believe that in Holy Communion
You give me Yourself —
Your Body and Blood, Soul and Divinity —
under the form of bread and wine.

In the Eucharist You are the Bread of Life.
Live in my soul and give me Your own life.
Give me the grace I need to do good
and to avoid all sin.

Continued on next page

Jesus, through the grace of Holy
Communion
help me to love people for the love
of God.
May I be kind to the people I meet
everyday
by helping them every way I can,
because You died for us all
and made us the children of Your
Father.

Through Holy Mass and
Communion
draw our family closer to Your
Heart
and lead us to heaven
to be with You forever.

Lord, I Offer You My Life

God, my Father,
may I love You in all things
and above all things,
and reach the joy
You have prepared for me in heaven.

Make me more like Jesus
through Holy Communion and prayer
that I may share in His glory
in His heavenly Kingdom.

Strengthen me in love,
and help me to serve You
in the people I meet each day.

Lord, I offer You my life
to praise and honor You.
May I always follow You
and do what You ask me to do,
that my whole life may give You glory.

Let the gift of Your life
of divine grace
make me always want to serve You
in faith, hope, and love.

Jesus, the dead body of a girl, twelve
years old, was lying on the couch. You
took her by the hand and spoke to her:
"Little girl, rise up!" And life returned to
the little girl. She opened her eyes and
sat up.

God, Thank You for Your Love

God my Father,
open my eyes to see Your hand at work
in the beautiful things You have made,
in the beauty of human life.

Gifts never stop coming to me
from Your goodness.
My life is Your gift.
Help me to live it well.
Guide me on my journey of life,
and keep me strong in Your love.

My God,
every good thing comes from You.
Fill my heart with love for You.
Give me a deep faith.
By Your loving care
protect the good You have given me.

Nothing is good which is against Your
     will.
Place in my heart a desire
to please You in all that I do.

Continued on next page

58

Father, help me to thank You
for Your many gifts around me.

Always be close to me
and hear my prayers.

Help me to be like Christ,
    Your Son,
Who loved the world
and died for our salvation.
Inspire me by His love
and guide me by His example.

May I always remain one with
    Jesus.
Give me the grace to follow Him
    more faithfully
and come to the joy of
    His Kingdom.

I Love You, Holy Trinity

Father,
You sent Your Son
to bring us truth
and Your Holy Spirit
to make us holy.
Through Them may we come to know You
  better.

Help me to worship You,
one God in three Persons, by living my faith
  in You.
One God, Three Persons,
be near to me.

Glory to You, God the Father,
my Creator, Who made me.
Glory to You, God the Son,
my Redeemer, Who died for me.
Glory to You, God the Holy Spirit,
Who make me holy.

My Dear Mother, Mary

Mary, Virgin Mother of Jesus,
and my dear Mother, too.
I give myself to you,
that you may protect me
and guide me to Jesus, your Son.

Keep me from all sin
that I may love Jesus
with a pure love
as you always did.

May I always enjoy
the help of your prayers,
for you bring us life and salvation
through Jesus Christ your Son.

I Praise You, God

Dear God,
I praise You, Father all-powerful.
I praise You, divine Son,
our Lord and Savior.
I praise You, Spirit of love.
One God, three Persons,
be near me in the temple of my soul.

You draw me by Your grace
to share in Your life and love.

I worship You, Eternal God!
I praise Your power and glory!
I praise Your mercy and love!

I believe in You,
I hope in You,
I love You, I adore You,
my God, living in my soul.

Keep me always close to You
and teach me to talk to You
    in prayer.

Lord, My True Home
is Heaven

Lord, You put me on this earth
to know and love and serve You
that I may be with You in heaven.

Lord, teach me to understand
that this world is passing,
that my true future
is the happiness of heaven;
that life on earth is short,
and the life to come eternal.

Help me to prepare for death
with a great trust in Your goodness.
Lead me safely through this life
to the endless joy of heaven.

Jesus, Walk With Me

God my Father,
You redeemed me through
   Your Son Jesus
and made me Your child.

Open my eyes to the wonderful
   things
this life sets before me,
that I may serve You
with all the love of my heart.

Receive the gift of myself —
all that I do or think or say —
and may my whole life give
   You glory.

Touch my heart with Your
   grace,
and help me to grow in Your
   love
and ever walk toward the life in
   heaven
You have promised.

Jesus, walk with me to heaven!

Other Great Books for Children

FIRST MASS BOOK—Ideal Children's Mass Book with all the official Mass prayers. Colored illustrations of the Mass and the Life of Christ. Confession and Communion Prayers.   Ask for No. 808

The STORY OF JESUS—By Father Lovasik, S.V.D. A large-format book with magnificent full colored pictures for young readers to enjoy and learn about the life of Jesus. Each story is told in simple and direct words.   Ask for No. 535

CATHOLIC PICTURE BIBLE—By Rev. L. Lovasik, S.V.D. Thrilling, inspiring and educational for all ages. Over 110 Bible stories retold in simple words, and illustrated in full color.   Ask for No. 435

LIVES OF THE SAINTS—New Revised Edition. Short life of a Saint and prayer for every day of the year. Over 50 illustrations. Ideal for daily meditation and private study.   Ask for No. 870

PICTURE BOOK OF SAINTS—By Rev. L. Lovasik, S.V.D. Illustrated lives of the Saints in full color. It clearly depicts the lives of over 100 popular Saints in word and picture.   Ask for No. 235

Saint Joseph CHILDREN'S MISSAL—This new beautiful Children's Missal, illustrated throughout in full color. Includes official Responses by the people. An ideal gift for First Holy Communion.
     Ask for No. 806

St. Joseph FIRST CHILDREN'S BIBLE—By Father Lovasik, S.V.D. Over 50 of the best-loved stories of the Bible retold for children. Each story is written in clear and simple language and illustrated by an attractive and superbly inspiring illustration. A perfect book for introducing very young children to the Bible.   Ask for No. 135

WHEREVER CATHOLIC BOOKS ARE SOLD

INDEX OF PRAYERS